I0086880

A SHAKESPEARE-INSPIRED TALE

Much

Ado

ART DIRECTION & TEXT BY NICOLE MALONEY

PAINTINGS BY TREG MILLER

MUCH ADO ©2011 by Nicole Maloney. All rights reserved.
No part of this publication may be reproduced in whole or in part, or stored in a retrieval system,
or transmitted in any form or by any means, electronic, mechanical, photocopying,
recording, or otherwise, without written permission of the publisher.

PUBLISHED BY 2M MEDIA, LOS ANGELES
©2011 by Nicole Maloney

ISBN: 978-0-9836433-1-9

*For information regarding permission, email Nicole Maloney at nicole@nicolemaloney.com
or visit the websites http://www.nicolemaloney.com or http://www.tregmiller.com.*

Much Ado, A Shakespeare-Inspired Tale is part of an entire series of Shakespeare stories and original paintings.
Other titles in print include: *Romeo Loves Juliet, A Shakespeare-inspired Tale.*
Titles available in 2012 include: *Hamlet, Henry V, Midsummer Nights Dream* and *Macbeth.*

Printed in the U.S.A.

Designed by Elisa Leone
THE PAINTINGS IN THIS BOOK ARE ORIGINAL ACRYLICS ON WATERCOLOR PAPER

FOR

KIDS OF ALL AGES

PUT THE BOOK DOWN AND DO TEN JUMPING JACKS

CLEAN YOUR ROOM

STOP EVERYTHING AND READ, READ, READ

SHAKESPEARE ROCKS!

THERE WAS A TALE OF DOUBLE-TROUBLE

THAT **LONG-LONG AGO** TOOK PLACE

WHEN DON JOHN'S EVIL FOIBLE

OOOOOOZED FROM HIS MOUTH AND FACE

EVIL DON JOHN TOLD SOME 'LIES'

TO SET HIS PLAN IN MOTION

LIES TO BRING ABOUT 'GOOD-BYES'

THAT CAUSED A HUGE COM-MMM-MOTION

IT WAS A MESS,
A FLOP-FLIP-FLOP
THEIR LOVE WAS TRUE,
A HOP-HIP-HOP

HE TRIED TO UNDO A NEW ROMANCE

PROFESSED BY THE WARRIOR CLAUDIO

WHOSE LOVE WAS SPARKED

AT FIRST GLANCE

FOR THE LOVELIEST LASS NAMED HERO

ALAS, THE 'LIES' TOLD BY THIS ROGUE

CREATED QUITE A RUMBLE-GUMBLE

THEIR COURTSHIP THAT HAD BEEN IN VOGUE

PLUNGED DEEP INTO A TUMBLE-WUMBLE

THERE WERE WHOAAA-BEEEE-GONE 'GOOD-BYES'

AS FORLORN CLAUDIO WAVED 'BYE-BYE'

LADY HERO WHOM NOBODY EVER CONSULTED

WAS LEFT TO WONDER AND SAY "WHY-WHY-WHY?"

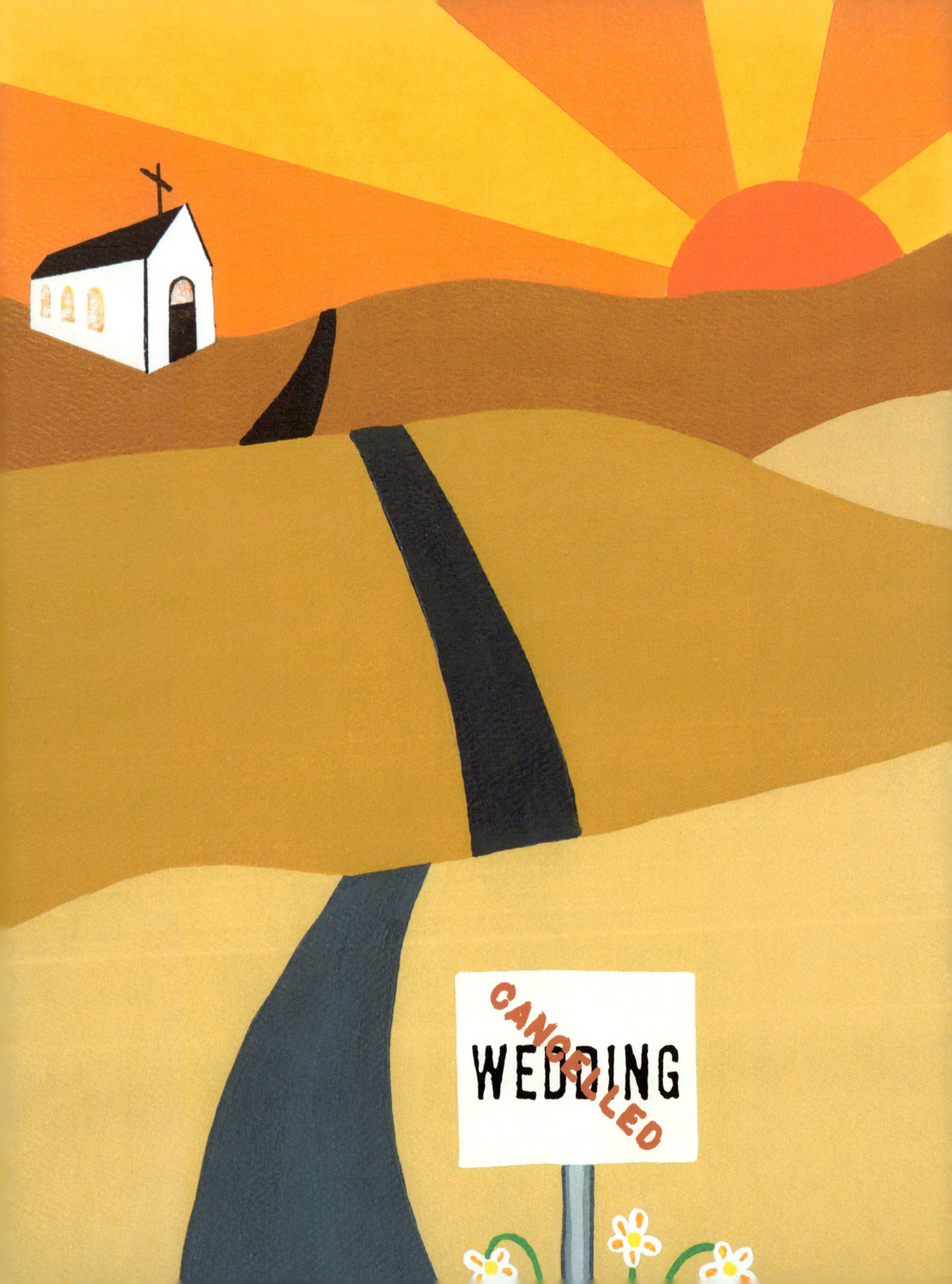

THE RUMORS AROUND

RAISED QUITE A FUSS

SO THE NEXT DAY'S WEDDING PLANS WERE NIXED

T'WAS SO MUCH WHIMPERING AND MORE FUSS

THEIR FRIENDS ARRANGED FOR IT TO BE FIXED

"IF WE CAN FOOL THE CROWD OUT THERE

AND HAVE THEM THINK HERO HAS

DIED-DIED-DIED

THE EVIL TALKER'S HEART MIGHT CARE

AND ADMIT TO ALL THAT HE INDEED

LIED-LIED-LIED!"

IT WAS A MESS,
A FLOP-FLIP-FLOP
THEIR LOVE WAS TRUE.
A HOP-HIP-HOP

DON JOHN CONFE

HIS EVIL

SO LOVE AND TRU

FOR HEARTS TO ME   ONE

THE COURTING OF CLAUDIO AND HERO RESUMED

AN ENGAGEMENT WAS ANNOUNCED

THEIR LOVE HAD NOW RE-BLOSSOMED AND BLOOMED

AS THE EVIL DON JOHN'S PLAN WAS TROUNCED!

HIP-HIP HORRAY!

HIP-HIP HORRAY!

HIP-HIP HORRAY!

THE END

MUCH ADO ABOUT NOTHING BY WILLIAM SHAKESPEARE

Much Ado About Nothing is a comedy interwoven with love, lies and evil trickery.
The story is centered on two couples: Benedick and Beatrice, and Claudio and Hero. Benedick and Beatrice
constantly argue and swear they have no love for one another. Claudio and Hero are so deeply
in love that they can barely utter words to one another.

The story is set in the beautiful Italian town of Messina to which Benedick and Claudio have just returned
from a victorious battle. Hero lives with her father, Leonato, the governor of Messina,
her cousin Beatrice, and her father's older brother, Antonio.

When Benedick and Claudio arrive at Leonato's home, Claudio is mesmerized by Hero and quickly falls in love.
On the other hand, Beatrice soon points out Benedick's ineptitude as a soldier and they are off in a war of witty insults.
Claudio is focused on being together forever with Hero. He asks for her hand in marriage. A week will pass prior to their
wedding day so to pass the time they all decide to play a game on Benedick and Beatrice. Benedick announces he will
never marry, but a match-making trickery is hatched to get them to stop arguing and fall in love. It is a success.

Sadly, not everyone is happy for the bride and groom. Evil Don John wants to destroy the wedding of Claudio and Hero.
Evil Don John leads Claudio to falsely believe that Hero has been unfaithful. Upon the wedding day, Claudio renounces
his love for Hero because of her supposed infidelity and embarrasses her in front of the entire wedding party.
Hero is dumb-struck and faints. Upon awakening, Leonato, her father, scolds her publicly. However, the Friar comes
to Hero's defense. He believes the Evil Don John is telling lies. The Friar hatches a plan of his own to reveal the truth.

The Friar convinces Leonato to fake Hero's death in hopes the Evil Don John will reveal the truth.
In the meantime, Beatrice asks Benedick to avenge Hero by slaying Claudio.
He refuses at first, but later challenges Claudio for insulting Hero, his lover's cousin.

Leonato ultimately blames Claudio for Hero's death and he too challenges Claudio to a dual.
Being the good man, Benedick does the same. The evil Don John's lies and trickery are discovered
and Hero's innocence is revealed to all. Claudio realizes his mistake, but is grief-stricken because
he believes Hero is dead. To punish Claudio, Leonato instructs Claudio to marry his "niece", a "cousin"
of Hero's who looks almost identical to her. As the bride presents herself to Claudio she is revealed as the real Hero.

Claudio is in shock, but gratified he is marrying his true love, Hero. The celebration begins.
During this happy time, Benedick asks Beatrice to marry him. After some bickering, she agrees.
The messenger arrives with the news that Evil Don John has been arrested.

All's well that ends well.

The story of *Much Ado* is inspired by Shakespeare's famous play, *Much Ado About Nothing*

www.ingramcontent.com/pod-product-compliance
Lightning Source LLC
Chambersburg PA
CBHW041241040426
42445CB00004B/113

* 9 7 8 0 9 8 3 6 4 3 3 1 9 *